UNDERSTANDING CRACK-ERS

*A spiritual approach to comprehending
why some White people are so hateful*

MICHELLE HOLLINGER

UNDERSTANDING CRACK-ERS

A spiritual approach to comprehending
why some White people are so hateful

UNDERSTANDING CRACK-ERS
A spiritual approach to comprehending
why some White people are so hateful

Hollinger Publications, Inc.
www.hollingerpublications.com

Dedicated to Black People.

And my White brothers and sisters who use their privilege with sacred awareness.

Love

Is patient and kind

Is not arrogant or rude

Is not self-seeking

Is not easily angered

Keeps no record of wrong

Rejoices with the truth

Always protects

Trusts and hopes

Always perseveres

Love never fails

CONTENTS

INTRODUCTION

The people screaming the loudest about making America great again are the ones most responsible for its woes. White supremacists, Trump and his supporters, murderous cops, spiritually ignorant preachers, and other racists in positions of power are modern day equivalents of slaveowners, Jim Crow bigots and destructionists. They collectively block the country's ability to reach its fullest potential by misusing sacred energy to destroy people who are different from them.

They insist that by terrorizing and attempting to oppress Blacks, restricting women's rights to control their own bodies, blocking immigrants from entering the country, suppressing votes and taking other unethical, immoral, far too often violent actions to limit non-whites' access to the American Dream, they are somehow safeguarding the nation's foundation and cultivating a brighter future.

They consider themselves patriots. They consider themselves upholders of the Constitution. They consider themselves true Americans whose actions are for the good of the country.

They're actually crack-ers.

"Cracker" is thought to have its origin in slavery and describes bigoted White people hell-bent on traumatizing, demoralizing, humiliating, murdering and desecrating Blacks. It was also used as a descriptor for poor immigrants from Scotland and Poland who arrived in the United States hoping for a better life, but that's not the group I'm referring to on these pages.

While the people who currently fit that description are likely descendants of crack-ers whose actions were responsible for many heinous actions, my focus with *Understanding Crack-ers* is not to condemn. The world is well aware of the horrendous actions crack-ers have taken and continue to take. The same deadly behavior crack-ers engaged in a century ago is interchangeable with current atrocities.

In his October 21, 1890, address at the Metropolitan A.M.E. Church in Washington, D.C., Frederick Douglass was reacting to the attempts of southern Resurrectionists to limit Blacks' newly won civil rights.

"The true problem is not the Negro, but the nation. Not the law-abiding Blacks of the South, but the White men of that section, who by fraud, violence and persecution, are breaking the law, trampling on the Constitution, corrupting the ballot box, and defeating the ends of justice. The true problem is whether these white ruffians shall be allowed by the nation to go on in their lawless and nefarious career, dishonoring the Government and making its very name a mockery. It is whether this nation has in itself sufficient moral stamina to maintain its own honor and integrity by vindicating its own Constitution and fulfilling its own pledges, or whether it has already touched that dry rot of moral depravity by which nations decline and fall, and governments fade and vanish," Douglass shared over 130 years ago, but his words also ring true regarding the January 6, 2021 insurrection where modern day "white ruffians" acted the complete fool.

Crack-ers have been at it for a very long time. The asinine content flowing from the mouths of crack-ers would be laughable if it wasn't so dangerous. Their willingness to flat out lie about experiences everyone can plainly see is insulting and frustrating.

We know what crack-ers have done and continue to do. It's time to understand why.

To that end, *Understanding Crack-ers* is not about rehashing what crack-ers do, but to instead share my understanding of why they do it. The hyphen is an intentional delineation meant to inspire a different interpretation of the word that requires looking beyond behavior.

Therefore, I'm examining "crack-ers" from a spiritual perspective to explain why certain White people behave so abhorrently. I'm digging deeper and going beyond the surface to explore insights, ideas and epiphanies to try to make sense of the nonsensical.

The country has made tremendous progress since the first Africans were coerced into its collective consciousness more than 400 years ago, however, if not for crack-ers, America could be much further along in its ability to be all it's capable of being. We can march, protest, vote in record numbers and pray without ceasing, but unless and until crack-ers heal, America will not function anywhere near its truest potential.

The title of the book will surely ruffle feathers. I'm ok with that if it sparks conversations that could heal America. For crack-ers who actually read the book and examine its true intention, I pray they'll receive what I've written in the spirit in which it was written – LOVE.

The truth is crack-ers, like everyone else, are spiritual beings having this human experience; however, their unawareness of this truth is a huge factor in the horrific behavior they've been exhibiting for centuries. The truth is there is authentic power within them that is far greater than the pseudo power they wield in the name of hatred.

America would be in much better shape if crack-ers who are subconsciously seeking relief from what has to be an exhausting existence were brave enough to examine who they really are and will finally allow the innate goodness within them an opportunity to reveal itself, for their good and for the good of the country.

Maya Angelou said, "when you know better, you do better." That's true for most people, some crack-ers included. I honestly believe crack-ers can do better.

But what I also believe is this: when Black people understand who crack-ers really are and why they behave the way they do, we can transmute the enormous amount of energy we expend on dealing with them and use it to manifest the lives we're meant to live.

Our presence here is by Divine order and we all have the power to make America great.

Chapter 1

WHAT IS A CRACK-ER?

In his August 1963 "Letter from a Birmingham Jail," Rev. Martin Luther King Jr. recounts how his then five-year old son, Martin III asked him, "Daddy, why do White people treat Colored people so mean?"

We may have graduated from being called "colored," but 59 years later, the question still needs an answer. Why *do* some White people treat Black people so mean? It's a question Black people have pondered for hundreds of years and continue to grapple with now.

Many have surmised that the White people inflicting atrocities upon Black people are just flat out evil, have hatred in their hearts and ice water running through their veins. Some believe that's just who they are and that they're destined to remain that way forever.

Actually, the White people inflicting atrocities upon Black people, members of the LGBTQ community, immigrants, Jewish and Indigenous people are not inherently evil. They are disconnected from their innate Truth. They have a crack in their consciousness that blocks their true essence as spiritual beings from informing how they show up in the world, hence the word *crack-er.*

(Black crack-ers exist too. Clarence Thomas, for example, is a Black crack-er married to his white counterpart. Black crack-ers have so thoroughly internalized crack-ers' messaging about them that they hate their own blackness and are aligned mentally and emotionally with white crack-ers.)

Crack-ers are unaware that they're spiritual beings and only function in the human dimension using their five senses. They are cut off from the richness of the universe because their ego keeps them myopically focused on what their eyes can see.

They've bought into the beliefs and stories passed on by their ancestors, and because epigenetics is real, they've acquired some of their beliefs through DNA.

Crack-ers actually believe they have the power to "make America great," because they're only focused on the physical aspects of living in the United States. They have no idea that spiritual energy informs material manifestations.

They prevent spiritual energy from blessing them and guiding them to their best lives by unwittingly using it to imprison themselves with nonstop externally focused, counterproductive behavior aimed at imprisoning others. They have no idea that the vile energy from which they spew hate towards others remains with them and shapes their lives.

Spiritual energy is impersonal and responds to the thoughts humans most consistently hold. Thoughts held in mind produce after their kind in ALL situations. There are no exemptions, spiritual law is as exact as mathematics and as predictable as gravity. $2 + 2$ will forever $= 4$, regardless of who works the equation. Gravity does its thing consistently, always responding objectively.

Crack-ers function predominantly from fear and anger. The way they think is full of a manufactured fear that they're being replaced, and the anger is a self-fulfilling rage stoked by people with something to gain by instigating and justifying crack-ers' dangerous behavior.

Most crack-ers do not realize the role fear plays in their lives, however, their awareness of its existence is irrelevant. If it has a predominant presence in their consciousness, it manifests in their reality. Crack-ers living solely from their human dimension have no idea that it's even possible to improve the way they live, in every aspect of their lives. They also have an irrational preoccupation with preventing or interrupting Black people from living their best lives.

So, seeing Black people eating drives them crazy. So does seeing Black people napping between study breaks. Black people walking their dog. Black people BBQing. Black people reading. Black people driving any kind of car. Black people living their lives fully and freely stirs up subconscious beliefs about who deserves what and is a painful reminder to crackers that they aren't living their lives to the fullest.

Think about it. A grown ass woman with the time, interest, and energy to report a little Black girl selling water is clearly not doing well. A person taking umbrage at Black men grilling food in the park ain't feeling so hot about herself. A person pretending to be under attack by a Black man minding his own business as he walks his dog is clearly off kilter.

What they all have in common is the distinct crack separating them from their innate spiritual nature. The most stubborn crack-ers have deeply entrenched beliefs about the source of their dissatisfaction with life. For centuries, the fallacy that African Americans and other non-whites impact their inability to live the American Dream has been so easily and pervasively used that it became a reality for crack-ers ignorant about their own spiritual truth.

Informed by the crack in their consciousness, poor White people have long had a convoluted perception of Black people that's fueled by self-serving fodder from richer White people who handle them like puppets.

In her book, *Masterless Men: Poor Whites and Slavery in the Antebellum South* Keri Leigh Merritt asserts that the enslavement of millions of Africans did a number on the

South's economy, politics, and culture in ways that often hurt poor White Southerners. Merritt pointed out that poor Whites were seen as a threat to the ruling planter class in the South because they jeopardized their profit margin.

Bacon's Rebellion is an example of a white power struggle that provided a glimpse of what might happen if White and Black people joined forces. It struck pure fear in the hearts of the White elite of Jamestown, Virginia when Nathaniel Bacon, a wealthy White property owner, galvanized a diverse coalition of White and Black indentured servants and Black slaves to attack Native American tribes in a battle for dominance that would allow him and others like him to expand their property. The militia was formed in defiance of the governor, who was afraid of antagonizing Native American tribes.

Michelle Alexander, the brilliant civil rights attorney and author of *The New Jim Crow* summarized the ramifications of Bacon's Rebellion:

"The events in Jamestown were alarming to the planter elite, who were deeply fearful of the multiracial alliance of [indentured servants] and slaves. Word of Bacon's Rebellion spread far and wide, and several more uprisings of a similar type followed. In an effort to protect their superior status and economic position, the planters shifted their strategy for maintaining dominance. They abandoned their heavy reliance on indentured servants in favor of the importation of more Black slaves."

They also realized how imperative it was to keep poor Whites hating Black people. Poor Whites' feelings about enslaved Blacks were a mixed bag of the typical hate based on the melanin in their skin. But it also included a warped dose of resentment because Black people, by being brutally enslaved and barbarically forced to provide free labor, were "taking" work away from impoverished White people.

The already foul mix of hatred and resentment was made even more maniacal, since by virtue of their whiteness and purported superiority, poor Whites were/are supposed to have easy access to the American Dream. The very people (rich Whites, politicians, etc.) who could (then and now) possibly provide poor Whites access to it are the very people needing them to remain enraged and therefore distracted from taking control of their lives.

They were/are the very people manipulating them into believing that their true enemy is the Black person, when in actuality, joining forces with Black people is likely their safest path to peace, joy and prosperity. They were/are the very people whose power gets usurped when/if poor White people start to think for themselves and become aware of their own power, their power as spiritual beings with access to unlimited abundance.

Imagine what it must feel like to have such dense, deadly, hateful vitriol constantly swirling within, occupying space intended for love. Making sense of it is futile so it's easier to align with what produces results, even if those results require constantly defying and numbing your most natural human impulses. (It's one reason excessive alcohol consumption is strongly encouraged in white nationalist groups.)

Seeing others suffer alleviates your own suffering when you're disconnected from your true essence. Dead Black bodies offer hollow solace. Cognitive dissonance requires the constant justification that "they deserved it," or some other concocted belief used to justify the unjustifiable.

The crack in consciousness widens when you believe you have no control over any other aspect of your life. Financial woes, health woes, relationship woes – all of crack-ers' woes are easier to ignore when the powers-that-be have not only given them permission to blame others, but routinely provide rationale for why they should.

In fact, as long as the majority of their existence is spent cultivating hatred, acting from hatred, destroying the country they claim to love by destroying fellow Americans, crack-ers have what feels like a legitimate excuse to not focus on their personal distress, which can feel insurmountable.

It's no coincidence that the majority of Trump's most ardent followers have not attended college. According to *The Atlantic,* prior to Trump's ascension to the presidency, "the single best predictor of Trump support in the GOP primary is the absence of a college degree."

This is not to cast aspersions on people without college degrees, however, a common thread has emerged as it relates to those most willing to blindly support Trump's rhetoric and do battle to destroy anyone who questions it.

The college experience is not simply a gauge of one's intellectual capacity, the college experience includes exposure to other cultures and races. It's a safe space for debating ideas and exploring others' points of view. It includes opportunities to expand one's perspective and process and perhaps challenge one's belief system. The greatest benefit of college is arguably its role in a person's development as a human being.

The economic consequences of not attending college are amplified if the people choosing not to pursue a college education do not invest in self-education.

According to *The Atlantic,* "Noncollege men have been trampled by globalization, the dissolution of manufacturing employment, and other factors, for the last few decades. In places like West Virginia, the mortality rate for middle-aged White men has grown since 1980, despite the fact that U.S. GDP per capita has quadrupled in that time. The causes are mysterious, but one outcome could be deep anger and political extremism manifested in Trump."

Crack-ers in higher socio-economic brackets aren't suffering financial frustrations like their poorer brethren. Their "sophistication" makes them less likely to resort to physical violence, but they use it to their benefit, nonetheless. They use their economic and political power to manipulate poor, uneducated Whites into carrying out the physical violence for them by keeping them drunk on hatred and intentionally inflaming their sense of powerlessness.

They understand poor Whites and are experts at speaking the language that taps into their fear and hatred. They cleverly engage poor Whites' personal hopelessness, not by offering solutions to improve their lives, but by providing the so-called reasons for it, perpetuating the powerlessness, stoking rage that masquerades as power.

They send out dog whistles that protect their personal and professional well-being while subtly inciting violence that masks their potentially criminal behavior. Lindsay Graham is the latest to employ this pathetic strategy by feigning concern that riots might occur if Donald Trump is indicted.

It's a part of the foundation of hate and contradictory thinking fomenting uncontrollably and manifesting in wanton hostility.

"I spent seven years in that world. A reality where I was constantly looking over my shoulder to reveal the handiwork of the enemy. Every aspect of our culture faced a relentless assault. Everything that was good about America – life, liberty and the pursuit of happiness – had been denigrated and disparaged by those that sought to impose Marxist equality," Arno Michaelis wrote in his remarkable book, *My Life After Hate*, which chronicles his life as a violent skinhead who eventually realized how wrong his actions were. "I hated (non-whites) for that. I hated them with the passion of a patriot. That hate was fueled by what I truly believed was a love for my race."

Waking up to the truth meant realizing that what he believed was "love for my race," wasn't love at all. The genuine love Arno now experiences illuminates that the "love for my race" white nationalism promotes is dangerous and counterproductive.

Crack-ers' twisted understanding of love is destroying America. It has for centuries and continues to do so in the 21st Century. What many might find hard to believe is that the absence of genuine love on the personal familial level and the resulting sense of unworthiness plays a humongous role in crack-ers' "love" for America.

Deeply entrenched unworthiness absent any awareness of innate spiritual nature prompts crack-ers to blame others for their woes and misfortunes. And because of its deep, centuries long festering, the belief that harming others or depriving them of rights crack-ers believe to be exclusively their own is continuously reinforced and validated.

Contemporary laws ostensibly forbid the type of barbaric, heinous and deadly behavior historically perpetuated against Black people, however, the same deeply entrenched unworthiness, unwarranted hatred and disconnection from spiritual nature spiraling uncontrollably in the crack-ers that killed Emmitt was the same deeply entrenched unworthiness, unwarranted hatred and disconnection from spiritual nature influencing the crack-ers that killed Ahmaud.

Fortunately, the crack-ers that killed Ahmaud are being held accountable for their actions and could, perhaps, from the sanctity of their cells, discover and mend the crack existing between their innate spiritual truth and the behavior that landed them there.

That type of unworthiness, hatred and disconnection from spiritual nature, mixed with the power to inflict harm on the perceived sources of crack-ers' misery produce barbaric, brutal, heinous and deadly behavior. It's that lethal combination that destroyed Black Wall Street and was behind every single massacre where throngs of crack-ers desecrated thriving Black meccas by declaring war on their fellow Americans, murdering them and destroying their property.

It was the type of unworthiness and severe disconnect fueling suburban mothers'/crack-ers' cruelty towards Black children integrating schools. It's the type of unworthiness and severe disconnect behind efforts to whitewash history books and classrooms by removing evidence of ancestral crack-ers' destruction of lives in the name of keeping America "great."

It's the type of unworthiness and disconnection from spiritual nature fueling crack-ers' attempt to overthrow a democracy by falsely claiming an election was stolen. It's the type of unworthiness and disconnection from spiritual nature pervading a U.S. president's consciousness that is responsible for how he pathologically lies, and intentionally manipulates disenfranchised crack-ers desperately blaming everyone else for their misery.

Donald Trump is the poster child for what happens when a crack-er is under the spell of deep unworthiness, is unaware of his spiritual nature and has access to unbridled power.

The crack-ers blindly following Donald Trump don't know how to take responsibility for their lives. They don't know that they can. He knows this so he preys on their powerlessness. What neither he nor they know is they possess innate spiritual power which can be used to manifest everything they say they want, and it has nothing to do with depriving anyone else of anything.

The same potent bewildering mixture of deadly, dysfunctional dynamics ruling poor Whites during slavery is the same concocted mentality ruling white nationalist groups today. Their mental health is under relentless assault by Trump and his band of political neophytes incapable of using their own intelligence to advance the conservative agenda that used to define the Republican party.

TYPES OF CRACK-ERS

Crack-ers don't just wake up one day hating everyone unlike them. Hate, anger, greed, resentment and the other low energy qualities crack-ers exude are not present at birth. They are learned behaviors crack-ers subconsciously agree to as a way of life. How they arrive at becoming a crack-er varies, however, the common denominator in all crack-ers' existence is the crack between their innate goodness that blocks it from shaping their perspective of themselves, others and life itself.

NASCENT CRACK-ERS

Most crack-ers learned their harmful beliefs and behavior from other crack-ers, who learned it from other crack-ers, and so forth and so on. The little White children holding their parents' hands as they watched Black people being lynched, standing there smiling like they just watched their favorite Disney character sing their favorite song were deeply damaged and emotionally scarred.

What they saw was horrific and patently unfair for their tender eyes to observe, but it was normalized by the adult crack-ers responsible for it. Witnessing human beings brutally attacked, a noose forced around their necks and asphyxiated as their bodies struggled for air until none was left became an everyday experience for school age children. These young children were unwitting crack-ers in training who very likely grew up to either become full blown crack-ers or people with severe mental health issues.

BENIGN CRACK-ERS

There are White people who have racist beliefs and hate Blacks and others who are different from them, but that's as far as it goes. They're benign crack-ers, crack-ers without the power to harm others and whose ideology only harms them. They're adults who throw hissy fits and pontificate about the merits of their whiteness when a company like Disney celebrates diversity by making a fictionalized character Black.

MALIGNANT CRACK-ERS

Malignant crack-ers brutally captured Africans and hauled them to America to be enslaved in the most dreadful ways. This group justified chattel slavery by buying into the concept of race, with theirs believed to be superior. They brutalized, raped, murdered and oppressed Blacks, based on their contrived belief in Blacks' inferiority.

Malignant crack-ers are card carrying members of the Ku Klux Klan, many of whom infiltrated police departments across the nation and used/use the uniform and badge as cover to destroy as many Black people as they can. Whether in the Klan or not, police officers murdering unarmed Black people are malignant crack-ers. Wanna-be-cops like George Zimmerman are malignant crack-ers, too.

Malignant crack-ers also wield violence in non-physical ways. They assault others' ability to function freely as citizens of this country. Republicans who suppress votes, advocate disparate sentencing guidelines, promote and profit from mass incarceration, and the myriad other tactics they employ to deny Black, Indigenous, brown, LGBQT and immigrant people the same opportunities they demand for themselves are malignant crack-ers.

COGNITIVE DISSONANCE

Crack-ers never, ever take responsibility for their actions. Crack-ers have gone to great lengths to salve the cognitive dissonance resulting from the crack in their consciousness separating the truth of who they are (spiritual beings) and their appalling behavior by conjuring up "research" they say confirms Black people are inferior and incapable of functioning intelligently.

Dr. Joy DeGruy, the brilliant social scientist and author of *Post Traumatic Slave Syndrome*, sums up cognitive dissonance this way: "Humans do not particularly like the discomfort that results when we commit a negative act or think about doing so."

She said we can resolve it one of two ways. One way is to own up to the negative act and address the harm caused by it. The other way is to justify the negative act rather than admit any wrongdoing. "'They deserved it," is a typical justification."

She adds, "In instances of particularly egregious negative acts, such as wars of aggression, enslavement, and genocide, the perpetrators have to go so far as to dehumanize and, in many cases, demonize their victims."

Arno Michaelis puts it like this, "Human beings naturally abhor seeing other humans suffer. The delusions inspired by fear and ego can cause us to dehumanize almost at will in order to justify that pain. Since we don't care to see our fellow humans suffer, we consciously take their humanity down a notch."

Additionally, crack-ers are entrenched in the falsehood that others can take what's theirs because they don't realize there is no competition in the spiritual realm and divine abundance means there's more than enough for everyone.

Seeing others who look like them behaving authentically, respecting and lovingly engaging others enrages them. Crack-ers refer to White people who live from their truth and treat others well as "race traitors."

The fascinating truth explaining their reaction to Whites who know who they really are and live lives that flow from that awareness is this spiritual truth: crack-ers would not feel anger unless they had the same qualities within them, qualities they never use because they don't know they exist.

Crack-ers are a sad bunch who can go their entire lives as imposters if they never go within to discover who they really are. Crack-ers with money and other material possessions falsely believe they're "successful." They're not if they engage in behavior that deprives, harms or in any way jeopardizes the liberty, well-being or dignity of others.

They are actually in bondage and peace of mind is elusive. They invite illness because thoughts and actions that do not align with their spiritual nature can begin to exact a physical toll on their bodies. They're also hostage to a preoccupation with acquiring money, often at any cost, (Joe Manchin) because they are fear-driven and ignorant of their innate prosperity and goodness.

Crack-ers are easily bought because they're either deeply divorced from or unaware that they possess innate integrity. This disconnect or ignorance makes it extremely difficult for them to cultivate their inherent ability to do the right thing. They get in so deep they know no other way to survive – so they remain in survival mode when an easier, more authentic approach to living is available.

Crack-ers are jealous of Black people who know they're free because it proves how powerless crack-ers are to actually oppress others. (For oppression to work, the people others are trying to oppress must agree that they're oppressed, think like they're oppressed and behave like they're oppressed. Fighting against oppression implies an acknowledgment that one is indeed oppressed.)

Black Wall Street enraged crack-ers because Black people had the nerve to manifest wealth and a joyful existence independent of crack-ers, who, ironically, could never experience wealth and a joyful existence as long as they're ignorant of their innate goodness.

Their sense of unworthiness – which they have no idea exists, making it even more dangerous – runs so deep they see others' success as a major threat to their existence and they spend inordinate amounts of time and energy attempting to strip other people of fundamental rights, including property and life itself.

18th century Swedish biological scientist, Carl Linnaeus was a crack-er known for his work with the taxonomic system that classifies plants and animals. He also took it upon himself to classify different types of humans. Mind you dude received a Ph.D. after one week for a thirteen-page dissertation from the Dutch University of Harderwijk, which had a reputation for selling degrees. Fake education and credentials notwithstanding, Europeans embraced his assertions as gospel because they needed something to legitimize their concocted belief in their superiority.

Crack-ers are disconnected from their innate worth, and when they're in positions of power they create policy, make rules, fabricate falsehoods and establish corporations and institutions that subjugate and exploit others.

Crack-ers in the political arena do a tremendous amount of harm to the country under the guise of patriotism. Ted Cruz is a crack-er. So are Marjorie Taylor Green, Josh Hawley, Ron DeSantis, Greg Abbott, Rudy Giuliani and politicians who see nothing wrong with police killing unarmed Black people while escorting white murderers to Burger King.

They don't operate from their truth, from their innate worth. They look outside of themselves to attempt to fill that void resulting from feeling unworthy. And because they're articulate and sound sincere to people desperate for guidance, their constituents keep them in office.

Even politicians dealing from the crack in their consciousness are shaped by unworthiness. They have endured life experiences that convinced them of their unworthiness, but instead of going to therapy to heal, they use their political skills to manipulate others and orchestrate grand schemes to get what they want.

Crack-ers have internalized oppressing others as a way of life. The longer they engage in various efforts to oppress others, the deeper the crack between the way they show up in the world via their behavior and the truth of who they are as spiritual beings.

Chapter 2

THE ROLE OF HATRED

Crack-ers are fueled by hatred and their hatred is born from fear. They feel obligated to hate others, which is not a natural part of their spiritual nature. Hatred is a learned behavior that is a part of America's foundation and continues to be a part of how it functions. It's passed down in crack-ers' generational patterns and via their DNA.

What crack-ers fail to realize is that their ability to hate others without reason could only stem from the hate they feel for themselves. Crack-ers are dealing with deep-seated self-hatred and are so disconnected from the truth of who they are that hating themselves and others comes easily.

To see a crack-er in full, unbridled hate mode, angrily spewing venom towards a complete stranger based solely on the person's skin color is to witness a human being so steeped in and controlled by self-hatred they literally cannot think straight.

Author and spiritual genius Gary Zukav explains, "When perception of the physical world is limited to the five-sensory modality, the basis of life in the physical arena becomes fear. Power to control the environment, and those within the environment appears to be essential."

Crack-ers have normalized hatred and go to great lengths to justify the maniacal behavior it produces by blaming others. Crack-ers blame others for not being like them. Crack-ers blame others for taking what crack-ers erroneously believe to be exclusively their own. Crack-ers blame others for simply existing.

Crack-ers have managed to institutionalize hatred so efficiently that despite laws forbidding it, some American corporations and institutions have cleverly incorporated hateful practices into their operational procedures.

Crack-ers are an example of people not knowing what they don't know because they're ignorant about the amazing goodness innately within them. They have no idea of the unlimited sacred qualities they were born with and became distanced from based on the family they were born into and/or the hateful experiences to which they were repeatedly exposed.

Crack-ers are victims themselves. Their ignorance robs them of an easier path to the life they say they want. They're puppets being controlled by people with something to gain from their blind allegiance to hatred.

Crack-ers are predominantly focused outwardly, incessantly searching for opportunities to reinforce the hate they feel towards others, however, their hatred is ingrained in their consciousness, in their minds and in their bodies. Of course, the pain they inflict upon others is harmful to the people they victimize, however, the people most harmed by crack-ers' hatred are the crack-ers themselves.

Everything about them suffers because they are completely unaware of and severely distanced from the inner splendor longing to be expressed. And because they're so mindlessly committed to harming or depriving others, they routinely fill silent moments with noisy reminders to hate.

Line up 100 crack-ers and ask if any of them have ever meditated and I'm willing to bet good money that no one will answer in the affirmative. It's impossible to be a crack-er if you meditate and tap into the vast field of love, peace and joy we're all born with.

A crack-er's subconscious is filled to overflowing with beliefs, attitudes, memories and experiences that inform the inaccurate perspectives they hold about others and justify the destructive actions they take to support their inaccurate perspectives. If they've had one experience they believe confirms their stereotypical perceptions about Black people, that one experience will color their beliefs about all Black people and will be mentally revisited time and again to reinforce their destructive behavior.

Crack-ers with ambition and high intellect misuse it when they conjure up belief systems that perpetuate the life of crack-ers and create vehicles for oppression and manipulation. If they align with their innate goodness, they can use their intellect to create policy, rules, laws, etc. for the benefit of all – not just for crack-ers.

They can use that intellect to receive downloads from Source, ideas that truly help America become great. Instead, crack-ers like Donald Trump are in low vibrational survival mode looking to fatten their already fat pockets and enhance their own lifestyles at the expense of others. They don't know they could manifest richly and abundantly if they tapped into the Source of their intelligence.

They don't realize that the ability to generate riches is easier when they heal the disconnect and align with their spiritual nature. They can discover that abundance is actually their birthright and does not require preventing others from experiencing theirs.

Crack-ers' inner turmoil is the reason for their selective amnesia, deep hypocrisy and willingness to violate spiritual law by rewriting manmade laws to suit themselves. Crack-ers blindly attacked the FBI's August 2022 raid on Donald Trump's home because it was another opportunity to demonstrate their allegiance to someone who helps them justify being a crack-er. It's another chance to join with the mind-numbing collective crack-er consciousness giving the finger to common sense, morality and independent thinking.

Chapter 3

ALL WHITE PEOPLE ARE NOT CRACK-ERS

In some Black circles, "cracker" is used to describe all White people. Sometimes used facetiously, sometimes seriously, however, when dumping all Whites under its label, the word is used stereotypically and unfairly. So, let's clarify which White people are crack-ers and which are not.

Slaveowners were crack-ers. Abolitionists were not.

Karens calling the police on innocent Black people are crack-ers. White allies using their privilege to facilitate justice and shine light on inequality are not.

White police officers looking for a reason to kill innocent Black people are crack-ers. White police officers getting to know the people in the community they patrol and treating them fairly, with dignity and respect are not.

Crack-ers are identifiable by their destructive behavior, disregard for human life and willingness to exist in a perpetual state of physical, verbal, mental or economic violence guised as self-preservation. Crack-ers operate from a deeply fragmented consciousness responsible for all manner of harm inflicted upon fellow Americans who don't look like them.

Crack-ers have no awareness of the wealth of goodness within them. Most believe they have nothing valuable to contribute to their families or society and genuinely think they are bankrupt in the gifts and talents department. They are suffering from a tremendous amount of self-loathing and a monumental degree of fear that they will never amount to anything.

Being offered what to them feels like a plausible excuse for their deficits – Blacks and immigrants are taking over –justifies wallowing in their powerlessness and victimhood. The belief system that there are limited resources, a finite number of jobs that non-whites are snatching up from America's "true patriots" legitimizes their anger and the violence they embrace in the name of keeping or regaining what they believe is rightfully theirs.

Crack-ers operate from a cracked space inside of themselves. They are not living from wholeness. They have no idea what it means to really love. The potential to love is within them, but it's smothered by dysfunction, falsehoods and hatred.

When it comes to the "love" crack-ers actually experience, Arno Michaelis explains, "Roads to a lot of really bad places are paved with that kind of bizzarro love. A vampiric, soul-depleting love-substitute that beckons to those who never know the real thing."

Crack-ers live from disillusion and self-loathing, masking both with righteousness and patriotism. But crack-ers don't have to remain crack-ers.

Understanding what makes them a crack-er offers insight and a life preserver for those interested in discovering who they really are and a roadmap to something better for those courageous enough to change their behavior.

Understanding crack-ers helps explain that crack-ers fall short on truly loving and respecting America because they don't know how to truly love and respect themselves. The "love" they proclaim for America isn't love at all. It's the out picturing of the massive disconnect from their innate being. It's a centuries old, extremely stubborn, very dense belief system held in place for so long that it feels correct and legitimate and untouchable.

Understanding crack-ers explains why they are obsessed with destroying others simply because of the color of their skin and why they believe their actions are justified.

Understanding crack-ers could engender hope and compassion among people who have washed their hands of dealing with wayward members of the American family.

Chapter 4

THE ROLE OF RELIGION

Religion plays a huge role in some crack-ers remaining crack-ers. Fundamentalists believe in a white god in the sky, a god in whose image and likeness they believe they were created. They believe the bible literally when it serves their interests and beliefs.

They believe that their god judges and punishes, and because they believe they were made in its image, they behave accordingly, judging and punishing others they believe to be inferior to them.

Crack-ers used religion to keep Black people enslaved, convincing them it was god's will for them to obey their masters. Many still believe that.

Many Blacks are still under the control of a colonized religion that kept their ancestors enslaved and often aligns with colonizers/crack-ers whose goal is to oppress them. Some Blacks are so deeply religious they're ignorant to its harm, how it limits them and makes them vulnerable to crack-ers' control.

Some Black churches have maintained the exact colonized religion, poured some soul into it and practice it faithfully to the detriment of their parishioners.

Many young Black people have abandoned their parents and grandparents' religion because they can clearly see the colonization running through it. Colonization their parents and grandparents are so accustomed to it has become a seamless part of their worshipping. They mouth things like "God, I ain't worthy," or "He didn't have to do it, but He did," the kind of contradictory nonsense crack-ers needed our ancestors to believe to keep them enslaved.

Some Black churches call out racism and white supremacy as evil and demonic. From a metaphysical perspective, they are because they represent separation from the Divine.

We are all spiritual beings having a human experience. Like gravity, it applies to all of us.

Interestingly, the spiritually empowering New Thought movement was birthed in the 1830s. It offers individuals an entirely different perspective on who they are (spiritual beings) and teaches people how to tap into their divinity to manifest greatness in every aspect of their lives. I can't help wondering how that movement might have influenced America had it been more widespread and readily accepted, but I digress.

Chapter 5

PROFESSIONAL CRACK-ERS

It's arguable that crack-ers are capable of wreaking havoc in *any* profession, but the five professions crack-ers absolutely inflict tremendous, life-changing damage in are as preachers, teachers, politicians, police officers and judges where the crack blocking their innate truth from informing how they behave comes into direct contact and influences the lives of others in large numbers.

Further, these five professions play such significant roles in shaping the country that as long as crack-ers occupy them, America will never reach its full potential. Consider each profession and how integral it is to how the country is run.

WHEN CRACK-ERS ARE PREACHERS

They preach unworthiness as a virtue and encourage a moral obligation to oppress, judge and punish. They find scripture to support their crackery and perpetuate a god in the sky concept that maintains congregations' disempowering belief in duality. Preachers were instrumental in sanctifying slavery, are instrumental in subjugating women and provide safe haven for crack-ers to hide behind religion.

WHEN CRACK-ERS ARE TEACHERS

They have the power to mold young minds. They reinforce in blossoming crack-ers the belief that they're justified to be a crack-er. They teach selectively to highlight historical information that supports crack-ers, while teaching non-white children they are inferior and deserve to be treated as less thans.

Crack-ers as teachers are especially lethal with young minds when they reinforce unworthiness by their treatment of young people whose trust in them is often absolute. Teachers are seen as authority figures whose wisdom often goes unquestioned by tender, impressionable minds.

Crack-ers as teachers wield a special kind of power that comes second to parents in its influence in shaping who a child becomes. Crack-ers as teachers keep school to prison pipelines busy, filled with young Black children who do not belong there.

Crack-ers as teachers are more likely to have energetic, bright, curious Black children sent to learning disabled classes than to have them tested for giftedness.

WHEN CRACK-ERS ARE POLITICIANS

They have the power to create policy and laws that govern the nation and the people residing in it. When crack-ers are politicians, they rule with a dangerous authority that is designed to keep certain populations under their control while providing their favored populations easier access to the country's resources. When crack-ers are politicians, they create policies and laws that legally subjugate others based on characteristics like skin color and sexual orientation.

When crack-ers are politicians, they scapegoat certain constituents, blaming them for historical institutional shortcomings like rusted pipes that pollute their water.

WHEN CRACK-ERS ARE JUDGES

They incarcerate innocent people based on the color of their skin and are instrumental in the manufacturing of modern-day slavery via mass incarceration. When crack-ers are judges, they abuse their power for the sake of punishing non-whites far more stringently than Whites and justify it based on their belief in Blacks being inferior.

When crack-ers are judges, young people like Kalief Browder sit in one of the most dangerous prisons in the nation for three years based on an accusation of stealing a backpack. When crack-ers are judges, their moral compass is non-existent, and the role is seen as an opportunity to legally destroy lives.

When crack-ers are judges, the black robe conceals a multitude of sins flowing from their crackery. When crack-ers are judges, their biases influence their rulings and they feign powerlessness when laws and regulations supporting their biases provide them pathways to act recklessly.

WHEN CRACK-ERS ARE POLICE OFFICERS

When crack-ers are police officers, unarmed Black men are shot and killed while doing any number of normal, day to day things while white murderers are coddled and taken to get fast food. When crack-ers are police officers, they use the gun and the badge as authority and license to kill, maim and wreak havoc in the lives of Blacks.

When crack-ers are police officers, certain people are treated as guilty, and the cops become the judge, jury and executioner. When crack-ers are police officers, they wield their power recklessly, shooting first, asking questions later. When crack-ers are police officers, they use the position to assassinate others with impunity.

When crack-ers are police officers, their unworthiness and power are most lethal since they are capable of actually killing someone and hiding behind the badge and "authority" provided them as officers.

When crack-ers are police officers, their reports are "revised" to support their lies. When crack-ers are police officers, "evidence" is conveniently planted in places guaranteed to support convictions or to justify lethal actions.

When crack-ers are police officers, they are complicit in their fellow crack-er police officers' misdeeds, cultivating the blue wall of silence.

When crack-ers are police officers, they instill deep fear in little Black children who view them as enemies instead of public servants hired to serve and protect.

Chapter 6

THE ROLE OF EVOLUTION

Every aspect of society evolves by releasing old ideas and replacing them with improved ways of being and doing. Modern technology has touched agriculture, medicine, education, law enforcement, entertainment, philanthropy and virtually aspect of society.

You name it and there is a newer, better approach to navigating everything we do. And that's how it is meant to be. Nostalgia is beautiful and has its place, but the past cannot be restored. In fact, people can pine for yesterday all they want, it's a spiritual truth that the past cannot be reinstated.

The Universe is timeless, intelligent, and progressive. Universal intelligence is a now reality. It doesn't function in the past or the future. Its vast unlimited availability is only accessible in the present moment.

We can't reach back and use Universal Intelligence to change the past and we cannot surge forward to craft a future. What we do now, in the present moment, shapes our future, but our energy can only be used now, in the present moment.

Universal Intelligence is unchangeable. It's constant and precise. Since the beginning of time, it hasn't shifted, however, humans' access to it has. As humans evolve, their ability to download brilliant Divine ideas gets easier and easier. The ideas are always there. The human mind, in its evolution, elevates and aligns with Divine Mind and allows humans to make the intangible, tangible.

In his brilliant book, *The Power of Decision*, Raymond Charles Barker says, "The Infinite is forever in the process of Self-Discovery. This Self-Discovery, individualized in man, is called evolution. We are the Infinite unfolding Its newly discovered aspects. Into our consciousness is pouring, at every instant, a flood of new ideas born of the Spirit, the Infinite Mind."

Evolution includes the manifestation of brilliant ideas meant to make life easier, more convenient and more enjoyable. Big, clunky cell phones that could only make an auditory call have been replaced by sleek, mind-blowingly magnificent smart phones that we use to surf the internet, video chat, take pictures, listen to music, write and read books, edit, make movies, play games, and the capabilities grow daily.

Traditional radios have been replaced by our ability to stream any song, from any era by the push a button or two or by telling Alexa to play it.

Medical advances that simplify diagnosing and treating patients, digital educational accessories that help teachers impart lessons, legal software that helps lawyers access case law within seconds and financial wizardry that manifests new forms of money are all normal manifestations produced by the evolutionary process. Infinite Intelligence needs human minds to take ideas from the invisible realm to visible, physical manifestation. Evolution is evident everywhere you look.

No area of life is left untouched by evolution because it's the natural order of things. We are meant to improve. Things are supposed to become easier. Life is meant to get better. Gary Zukav's exceptional *Seat of the Soul* asserts that "humans are evolving from a species that seeks power based on the perception of the senses to one seeking power based on spiritual values."

Anything standing in the way of evolution will be exposed and eventually there will be enough collective energy for transformation to occur. It's how slavery ended. It's how the Civil Rights Movement put an end to the Jim Crow era. And it's how the seeming epidemic of crack-ers wreaking havoc on the country will ultimately cease to be an issue.

Interestingly, people who insist on holding onto old, outdated ways of doing things can find themselves facing unnecessary obstacles. Life is harder than it has to be because of their unwillingness to let go of outdated ideas and approaches to living.

Evolution also impacts the intangible, which includes human behavior. Parenting styles are evolving and giving way to a gentler approach to raising children that is less punitive, healthier and more communicative.

Evolution has produced more humane approaches to navigating even stubborn institutions like the criminal justice and child welfare systems. Procedures like restorative justice and family team conferencing are effective tools that solve problems holistically. These types of processes include a shift from a purely penalizing approach that does little to impact underlying core issues to better practices that facilitate healing and growth. They are beneficiaries of the evolutionary process.

Despite crack-ers' desire to behave as their ancestors did, brutalizing people with impunity, evolution dictates otherwise. Rogue police officers have been getting away with torturing unarmed Black people for who knows how long, however, their behavior is being increasingly exposed thanks to the advancement of cell phones that essentially equips everyone with portable cameras.

The improvement of cell phones is not only for our convenience. Their function plays a significant role in the evolution of human behavior. Evolution dictates that crack-ers' horrific conduct be revealed so that sacred healing can occur, not just for the victims, but for the perpetrators, as well.

Crack-ers are preoccupied with the past and oblivious to the notion that America is not meant to continue placating their atrocious behavior. The evolution of technology is a necessary component that plays a vital role.

From a spiritual perspective, the 1991 video of police officers viciously beating a defenseless Rodney King was an evolutionary tool capable of facilitating widespread healing in America. King could have understandably been bitter and angry and could have used his platform to encourage vengeance. Instead, his soul spoke through him when he pleaded, "can we all get along?" The subconscious intention of that violent encounter was to produce peace and healing. It did not.

At the individual level, when humans do not heal underlying emotional issues that result in unpleasant circumstances, those unpleasant circumstances repeat. For example, a person in an unhealthy relationship will continue to attract different relationships with the same unhealthy dynamics until they heal their inner emotional patterns, whether it's unworthiness, low self-esteem, self-loathing or some other factor that is preventing them from showing up authentically.

At the collective level, the same holds true. When America is presented with unpleasant circumstances that amplify what needs to be healed, but no healing occurs, the unpleasant circumstances continue.

Twenty-nine years and many failed healing opportunities after the Rodney King assault, the video of George Floyd's murder was yet another powerful evolutionary tool that opened eyes worldwide and had an influence on racial healing. Witnessing for themselves something Black people have been enduring sans videos was necessary for millions of people to finally realize what crack-ers have been up to.

Derek Chauvin's cavalier attitude, hands in his pockets as he casually snuffed a man's life from his body was reminiscent of Jim Crow era brutality from White men who knew their behavior would go unquestioned and unpunished. The disbelief that something so barbaric could still be occurring was centered on the assumption that humans have evolved significantly enough that such behavior could no longer happen.

There seemed to be a radical shift occurring. White allies marched in Black Lives Matters protests, began to support Black-owned businesses and made attempts to use their privilege to help correct some of America's wrongs. However, because those interested in solving the problem attempted to solve it at the level of the problem, nothing lasting manifested.

People were sincere, but since the progress did not include widespread healing with crack-ers; did not involve introspection to understand the underlying reasons for the depraved behavior or any collective healing efforts, crack-ers continue to act out from a twisted mix of unworthiness, fear, anger and resentment.

Unless and until crack-ers mend the crack that separates them and their behavior from their intrinsic goodness, and begin to live from that sacred space, they will continue to inflict murderous harm upon others, some of which will be captured on camera.

The continued defiance of their natural evolutionary process is a stubborn trait exasperated by fear. Crack-ers are meant to evolve as well, however, they stifle their own growth and development in their misguided effort to "make America great again." In order to reclaim the America they're hoping for, major regression must occur. In order for crack-ers to wield the type of deadly power their ancestors wielded, civility must be discarded along with any strides in racial and social justice.

In order to take America backwards and return it to a country that only allows a select group of its citizens to enjoy life, liberty, and the pursuit of happiness, crack-ers must continue to actively ignore the evolutionary impulses pulsating within them. They must disregard any inkling to be and do better and actively embrace the maniacal degradation and murderous behavior their ancestors displayed during Black massacres across the country. They must continue justifying the unpatriotic foolishness that occurred on January 6, 2021, and they must play dumb each time a police officer chooses to kill an unarmed Black person instead of treating them with the respect and dignity they routinely show White suspects, some wielding weapons.

Evolution does not skip over crack-ers. As spiritual beings having this human experience, the opportunity to become better versions of themselves is as readily available to them as it is to anyone. And the "better" is a version of themselves they would feel good about.

It's a version of themselves that would nullify the need to harm anyone else. It's a version of themselves that would lift them from their stupor of denial because they'd finally be standing in their truth and becoming familiar with authentic power. They'd be amazed at how much easier life actually becomes.

But crack-ers are largely unaware that this inner impulse is in their best interest and could lead to an elevated consciousness manifesting wonderful experiences that seem impossible for them to attain.

Denial is a major aspect of a crack-er's existence. And hypocrisy. And enough contradicting beliefs to cloud and prevent their minds from accessing Infinite Mind and receiving the unlimited greatness constantly flowing from it.

It takes a tremendous amount of energy to prevent evolution from occurring in your life. It's like trying to push hair back into your scalp. Defying evolution results in a stubborn and irrational embrace of the status quo. It's a self-defeating surrender to mediocrity, a constant effort to silence the inner voice whispering, "you're better than this."

Each person's soul is here to fulfill a mission. Everyone is born on purpose, with a purpose. A soul's primary purpose is to express Divinity and the secondary purpose is the expression of unique gifts and talents. The expression of those gifts and talents is often how each person expresses the Divine. In addition to the expression of unique gifts and talents, some souls are here to help elevate the collective good for humanity.

If you're not familiar with the mission of souls and their role in the evolutionary process, the idea that George Floyd's soul and Derek Chauvin's soul conspired for that moment as a part of something far larger than either of them sounds ludicrous. On face value, it was an inhumane, vicious, sadistic murder, but from a spiritual perspective, both men's souls were complicit in that devastating encounter. So was the soul of Daniella Frazier, the brave young woman who recorded it. It was no coincidence that she and her young cousin were there at the precise time Chauvin murdered Floyd.

"Even though this was a traumatic life-changing experience for me, I'm proud of myself. If it weren't for my video, the world wouldn't have known the truth. I own that. My video didn't save George Floyd, but it put his murderer away and off the streets," shared Frazier, who was 17-years old at the time. What she doesn't realize is that her actions not only put his murderer away, but also played a very significant role in evolving collective consciousness regarding racism.

When George Floyd's baby girl exclaimed that her daddy was changing the world, her words were true in myriad ways. The evolution of human behavior requires improvement. Evolving human behavior in hostile, resistant beings ignorant about their role in the collective improvement of the world happens in difficult, often painful situations, but evolution cannot be stopped.

Crack-ers certainly believe something to the contrary, but their base, animalistic desires will not prevail because even their extreme violence pales in comparison to Divine power.

Eric Garner, Sandra Bland, Philando Castile, Michael Brown, Yvette Smith, Rekia Boyd, Alton Sterling, Tamir, Rice, Walter Scott, Breanna Taylor, Ahmaud Arbery, Andre Hill, Eurie

Martin and many, many more souls contributed to the evolutionary process by being a part of viscerally painful experiences that could ultimately help facilitate collective healing.

The murderers thought their hateful actions were aimed at destroying Black lives, but the souls of the crack-ers responsible for these deaths were complicit in creating healing opportunities for this country. Souls' missions often differ from what their human hosts anticipate and can fully comprehend. The lessons left behind are for the living, who get to help complete the souls' missions. We get to make certain these precious souls' missions are accomplished and their deaths were not in vain.

Chapter 7

REFORMATION

Can crack-ers change? Absolutely. Being a crack-er is not who they really are, so returning to their truth, to the essence of who they are as spiritual beings is absolutely possible.

The perfect example is the grandparent who was racist their whole life, raised that way and continued well into their senior years. Then their child has a baby with a Black person and that grandchild's love penetrates the crack in the grandparent's consciousness that was blocking the grandparent from the love in their own heart and soul.

This potent love resonates because it connects with the truth of who Grandpa is, and it restores him to himself. Try as he might, he can't deny it. The change happens inside first when he experiences the child's love, a reflection of the love deep within him.

The relationship between that child and the racist grandparent becomes a sacred bridge transporting the grandparent to experiences he/she could not reach on their own. A huge part of their transformation occurs because the child's pure untarnished love sees them, not as a crack-er, not as a racist, not as a white supremacist; it sees them as who and what they really are. They are seen as LOVE.

The tiny sliver of light gets in, resonates and allows them to feel something they'd denied themselves. The child's pure love has a profound healing effect on the crack.

Those who talk about it publicly realize that not only are they saving their own life, but by speaking openly, even if they reach just one other person with a crack in their consciousness, they can save that person's life even if that person has not had the firsthand experience of pure love.

That person could still experience its benefits because it's also the truth of who they are. When the student is ready, the teacher appears. And this learning experience shines a mirror that informs them of their ability to give and receive love.

When people with a crack in the consciousness get a glimpse of their spiritual nature, they can shift from the most rudimentary aspect of their existence, victimhood, the first of four stages Michael Bernard Beckwith created to help people understand the different dynamics of their spiritual nature.

Beckwith, one of the most brilliant men on the planet and founder of Agape International Spiritual Center in California, created the "Four Stages of Spiritual Growth and Development" in the mid-1980s to provide a useful and enlightening perspective on the journey from victimhood to empowerment. The four stages help anyone interested in personal and spiritual development to better understand where they are and what they can do to progress through the stages.

As it relates to people with a crack in their consciousness, the four stages illuminate how unawareness of their spiritual nature keeps them mired in the lowest level, and how healing the crack positions them to experience higher levels of spirituality.

People with a crack in their consciousness have no idea that there are opportunities for spiritual growth because they don't realize they're spiritual beings. If they become aware of their spiritual nature, healing the crack and advancing through the developmental stages becomes far more feasible.

People with a crack in their consciousness are immersed in the first stage, the "To Me," victim stage. In this stage, people move through the world believing that some external force or power is controlling their life. They are far more likely to blame others for what's wrong with their life and may catch themselves saying something like, "Why does this always happen to me?"

People with a crack in their consciousness believe life just happens and it's necessary to deprive others to enhance their own ability to have the things and experiences they say they want. That way of life is severely limited and deeply rooted in a "woe is me" mentality.

People in this stage are unable to see that they have access to a power for good in the universe that is greater than they are, which they can use. It is a disempowering context through which to live and people with a crack in their consciousness resort to other ways to feel powerful, like violence.

People with a crack in their consciousness spend an inordinate amount of time in stage one. A person's age has little to do with which stage a person is in. Anyone aware of their inner power can move through the stages with ease and grace, arriving at the third and fourth, "Through Me" and "As Me" stages and do tremendous work for the planet.

Some people, like Blake Mycoskie, seem to exude the third and fourth stage effortlessly. The 46-year-old social entrepreneur is abundance and goodness personified because he is tapped into his spiritual nature and accesses Infinite Intelligence as a matter of course to guide his service to the planet.

Conversely, Donald Trump is 76-years old and still in the stage one "To Me" victim mentality, harming others because he doesn't realize who and what he really is. If he or other people with a crack in their consciousness ever discover they're not a victim, that other people cannot take from them what is theirs by divine right, and no one is doing anything to limit them, they can elevate and discover that the world is not happening to them, but "For Them" in the next stage.

The love of his daughter, his hopes and dreams for her and the love and kindness shown him by people he hated all factored into Arno Michaelis' elevation from the victimhood stage. He's such an amazing example of what happens when the crack is mended.

"We all have the ability to realize our basic human goodness – the innate and natural desire to live an open and honest life while treating all other life with compassion and respect. This core truth serves as the foundation for peace as it's common to every world religion and transcending of ethnicity, nationality, sexuality and any other sort of difference that seems to sort human beings," he said in his book, where he acknowledges that leaving hate behind and replacing it with love takes work but is worth the effort.

"Once we choose to take that path, and persevere along its drastic ups and downs, we're able to recognize the true beauty of life. The path that seemed so treacherous becomes joyful and rewarding as we soothe our own suffering by simply loving our great big dysfunctional family – the human race."

One practice that Arno has incorporated into his life is meditation, a beautiful way to heal the crack and discover one's authentic self. The answer to healing the crack is within, and meditation allows people to touch the divine, where the window into the soul's vast goodness exists.

The stage two "For Me" phase blesses people healing the crack in the consciousness because by realizing they're powerful vessels through which a Higher Power can manifest, they begin to feel empowered and capable of co-creating what they desire, instead of being used by people with ulterior motives. The hopelessness and frustration that fueled their attraction to white nationalist groups begins to dissolve under the light of clarity shining brighter and brighter in their lives.

The second stage is all about manifestation. Donald Trump has experienced this stage because he's a master at manifesting. He knows how to use his thoughts and words to generate success and huge amounts of money, but because of the crack in consciousness, he also uses this power to manifest mayhem.

People in the third "Through Me" stage of spiritual development, have completely healed the crack in their consciousness. They let go of control and the illusion of power. They're encountering others who have healed, and it feels good to surrender the need to control every aspect of their life.

They're no longer reactive and now examine and question dictates instead of blindly following commands that harm others. They move into the flow of life, becoming an instrument of the Divine as they continuously surrender to the Indwelling Presence.

In this stage, they may receive nudges from the Divine to move in a specific direction, or they may get shoved if necessary. They have the consciousness of, "I surrender, I am an instrument, I am a vehicle through which Spirit speaks and acts." Life is happening through them.

When people evolve into the fourth "As Me" stage, they are no longer recognizable to people who knew them when/if they had a crack in their consciousness. Evolution into the fourth stage means ideas of separation lose their power.

The love in them sees the love in others. Hate has no place at all. Through the consistent yielding to Source Energy, the Divine takes the driver's seat in life. The last vestiges of ego and separation dissolve.

People fully immersed in the fourth stage move through life completely aware that they're spiritual beings and intentionally and easily allow Spirit to express as them. It is impossible for the foolishness that pervaded their consciousness when they were in the first stage to manifest now.

They are fully capable of feeling deep compassion for others who are still suffering from the crack in their consciousness. The fourth stage is that of unity. At this point, they experience Spirit as themselves. In the flow, people are called to trust and be.

Although the four stages are a great roadmap for people with a crack in their consciousness to discover their spiritual nature and understand their journey, the stages are beneficial awareness of anyone's spiritual development. As it relates to Black people, those operating at stages three and four are best suited to thrive.

Chapter 8

RADICAL FORGIVENESS

The African American influence on the nation is unmistakable. Our presence on the planet is not coincidental but by Divine Design. Our culture, our style, our vibe, every wonderful thing about us shapes this country and the world. Our very essence is contagious and exudes a soulful frequency emanating from everything we do.

If we intentionally focused our energetic vibration towards healing this country, we would be surprised at what happens.

We have the power to do so and it is extremely possible. To that end, the real work required to create a country that works for everyone involves radical forgiveness and intentionally sending people with cracks in their consciousness love and positive energy.

This idea to help facilitate widespread healing is multifaceted because it also plays a monumental role in Black people improving how we access our own unlimited power. It goes a long way to manifesting safe environments for black and brown bodies to live freely just like everyone else. It is, I believe, our best hope for significantly reducing the maliciousness that seems to grow stronger each day.

The lyrics to Hezekiah Walker's beautiful song "I Need You" are perfect. I knew just how perfect they were when, while blasting the song and singing along, Donald Trump's face surprised the hell out of me when it popped into my mind, evoking emotions I truly did not expect. I prayed for him in that moment. I have prayed for him before and will continue to pray for him often.

Blacks willing to engage in radical forgiveness as it relates to people healing their cracked consciousness are not only contributing to energy that could transform the country, but importantly, we're also giving ourselves a tremendous gift that pays rich dividends in our own lives.

Forgiveness benefits the forgiver by setting them free. By releasing them from being hostage to a situation over which they have no control. Forgiveness is good, but Radical Forgiveness is even better. It takes it to a higher level.

Radical Forgiveness operates on the belief that we're all spiritual beings and our encounters are rooted in our spiritual nature. It posits that experiences have an underlying spiritual intention and when the parties impacted by the experience are open to discovering the unique purpose of the experience, they can view it as "a blessing in disguise."

Applying Radical Forgiveness to racial dynamics is delicate because any implication that slavery, Jim Crow and all the atrocities inflicted upon Black people were blessings of any type sounds insane. That's not the intention, at all. The intention is to take an otherwise dense, seemingly unforgiveable atrocity and find the sacred in it so that it no longer blocks us from thriving.

It is choosing to view it differently. It is allowing yourself to be free of stagnating energy that prevents vibrant energy from flowing in, through and as you. Forgiveness wipes anger and resentment from your eyes so that you can see yourself and the world anew.

Black people participating in this collective forgiveness process will unblock sacred energy in their personal lives, opening valuable space for more goodness, joy, health, love and abundance to manifest. That saying "not forgiving is like drinking poison and expecting someone else to die," is absolutely on point. It feels justified and perhaps productive to examine the ways crack-ers are wrong, seemingly evil and how they'll never change, however, the energy surrounding those thoughts remain in the thinkers' minds.

Each time a crack-er is caught on camera brutalizing a Black person, the anger, deep exhaustion and resignation that things will never change is a natural response, however, it helps ensure that things will never change if the sentiment stops there. Anger is a healthy response but one that must be processed and moved beyond. Allowing it to be the only and final response is incomplete in the radical forgiveness process.

Black people being able to excel despite the overwhelming presence of dehumanizing, often violent efforts to destroy them is evidence of their ability to take the lead on healing this nation. When crack-ers heal, the nation heals, but Black people play a key role in that healing process. Black people are not responsible for healing the cracked consciousness, but we play a key role in it helping to make it happen by expecting it to.

The collective consciousness sustaining crack-ers' hold on the country is fueled by separate factions. Crack-ers themselves have a stubborn, dense, seemingly impenetrable consciousness of hatred, oppression, barbaric, irrational behavior solidified by centuries of crack-ers living solely from the limited human dimension where hate can flourish. That coagulated consciousness is immensely powerful, in part, due to the sheer number of crack-ers holding it as their truth and the astounding length of time it's been embraced as gospel.

Crack-ers continue to behave in mind-boggling fashion. Still acting from their warped belief in superiority and entitlement. Frustrating as hell to witness and even more demoralizing and devastating to experience, however, Blacks, immigrants and other targets of crack-ers' wrath unwittingly contribute to the consciousness that sustains crack-ers' negative hold on the country by responding to their negativity with negativity, even if the negative responses are simply thoughts and words.

Blacks have normalized this perception of crack-ers, in part, to survive living in a country where racism is rampant, institutionalized and showing no signs of being eradicated. Blacks expect crack-ers to be crack-ers and have adjusted accordingly.

In sociology, collective consciousness (sometimes called collective conscience or consciousness) refers to a set of beliefs, ideas, attitudes, and knowledge that are common to a social group or society as a whole. Collective consciousness can and does change behavior. Collective consciousness is extremely powerful and can sustain or transform according to its most potent intentions.

Fighting against crack-ers, while necessary in some situations as a matter of life or death, expends a tremendous amount of energy that inadvertently contributes to their sustainability; not because Blacks *want* crack-ers to wreak havoc, but because spiritual law is impersonal and works with mathematical precision all the time.

"Thoughts held in mind, produce after their kind," "Where your attention goes, energy flows," and" What you think about, you bring about" are spiritual principles that manifest tangible results. It does not matter what the subject matter is, what you most think about manifests into reality.

So, although it's understandable that after centuries of crack-ers behaving as though they were only vile, evil monsters, the targets of their venom would come to view them as such, the vast energetic frequency inherent in Blacks' collective consciousness joins with crack-ers' consciousness and maintains their flawed existence. In other words, by responding to their low vibrations with low vibrations, we contribute to the continuation of their low vibrations. Countering hatred with hatred, keeps hatred alive.

There's a different, far more beneficial way to respond that can ultimately save Black lives. Studies have documented the effectiveness of groups of people meditating for an intended result. Years ago, an experiment using Transcendental Meditation was facilitated with the goal of reducing violent crime, with great outcomes. Violent crime was significantly reduced when a very small percentage (square root of one percent) of the population participated for a designated time frame.

"I understand it's a new hypothesis in the social sciences that meditation could have a stress-reducing and coherence-creating effect in society," said lead author Michael Dillbeck. "But such research is increasingly suggesting that there's a field effect of consciousness. If you get a large enough group together practicing this technique to experience the field quality of consciousness, these extended 'field-like' effects are expressed in society."

Although this experiment used a specific technique, Transcendental Meditation, I strongly believe that if a large enough group of people committed to something as simple as thinking specific positive thoughts about people with a crack in their consciousness at a designated time each day for a designated length of time, it would have a powerful effect on America's collective consciousness.

On an individual basis, one person can shift their perception of someone with whom they interact on a regular basis and change the dynamics of the relationship. One person can, by consistently seeing the best in their partner for a long enough timeframe, encourage that person to behave differently without saying a word to them about changing their behavior.

As it relates to how Black people treat, interact with or respond to crack-ers, it's important for them to recognize that crack-ers are wounded and living from their wounds. The way crack-ers behave is not normal. It helps to view them as you view a wayward cousin for whom establishing healthy boundaries is essential.

The frustration family members feel about that cousin is similar to the frustration Blacks could feel about crackers. And the same way families refuse to give up on the cousin, even if their antics land them in hot water, Blacks must become willing to extend the similar grace to crack-ers – from a safe distance, if necessary.

Even crack-ers who have behaved heinously have done so from the large crack separating them from their innate spiritual nature. They were not in their right mind. That includes those who took the life of innocent Black people.

It's important for Blacks to hold space for crack-ers to heal, realign with their truth and it's important for Blacks to want the best for them. As long as Blacks engage and match crack-ers' low energy, it's solidified and we unwittingly motivate crack-ers to dig their heels in deeper to protect their cause. Michelle Obama's encouragement, "when they go low, we go high," is even more powerful when you understand the spiritual ramifications of collective energy.

Arno Michaelis is a White man who used to be crack-er. He's not anymore. He was once a racist skinhead who co-founded one of the largest white nationalist organizations in the country. Arno has mended the crack between his spiritual nature and how he shows up in the world. He's doing amazing work to help crack-ers heal.

He speaks freely about his past to help people understand how terribly flawed his perspective was and essentially confirms *Understanding Crack-ers'* premise that racists are not in touch with the best part of themselves, severely disconnected from the spiritual nature and floating in a sea of unworthiness.

Arno explained in his book that he and his comrades lived for conflict and confrontation. They thrived on the angry responses they elicited by wearing racist garb and displaying arms covered in swastikas and other hateful rhetoric in public. They relished any opportunity to brutalize others who dared confront them.

People who defied his hate by showing him and his peers love and kindness took the wind out of them because it did nothing to ignite or exacerbate their rage. It did nothing to legitimize their hatred or reinforce their stereotypes about Blacks or Jews or gay people.

Arno said he expected the people he hated to hate him in return, but when they showed love and kindness, their goodness seeped beyond his tough persona and landed in unfamiliar spaces within him.

One of the stories he shared in his book made me burst into the big cheesy grin because it so accurately reflects how genuinely loving Black people can be. Arno said he'd been out the night before drinking and raising hell. Nursing a hangover the next day at work, a Black co-worker saw that he was struggling, addressed him as "skinhead," and offered him half of his sandwich.

He had no idea how to navigate such behavior, but eventually, with enough of it in his subconscious, it began to replace some of the vitriol taking up space there. He credits the birth of his daughter as well as those acts of kindness as instrumental in his transformation from a brutally racist skinhead into a man on a mission to help the nation heal from its racist hatred.

Arno said responding in kind to a violent racist only fuels his behavior. Responding with love is easier said than done but is the only response that can penetrate the part of him where love exists and could ultimately promote the kind of healing Arno experienced.

I believe these acts of kindness are cumulative and could eventually take up so much space in a person's subconscious that they begin to shift their perspective. I believe when a person is healing the crack in their consciousness, that one "random" act of kindness could be the catalyst that removes their blinders of hate and allows a sliver of love in.

Love is the only answer. Agape love. Love that surpasses human understanding. Love beyond five sensory comprehension. The kind of love Jesus talked about, but most people misunderstand. Unconditional love. Big love. Deep love.

And Black people are full of love.

We've been criticized for being so willing to forgive crack-ers who have killed loved ones or done other monstrous acts. We're quick to forgive because we know subconsciously that it's essential to our own healing.

Forgiving is a critical ingredient in crack-ers' healing, however, the quick forgiveness some Blacks have offered publicly is well intended, but rings hollow. It's not what facilitates the type of healing that really helps Black people excel and it's not what America requires to reach its greatness.

It has the right idea but lacks the substance resulting from processing the anger and hurt that are natural and necessary parts of the grieving process. So, yeah, forgiving is great, but doing the work that extends it beyond lip service is far more beneficial for all involved, especially the forgivers.

Nevertheless, Blacks are willing to forgive, which is an essential part of crack-ers mending the crack, discovering who they really are and genuinely giving up the desire to destroy others. The goal is not to achieve some kumbaya moment where we're all holding candles and singing "We Are the World."

Nice, but the real work might or might not result in interracial friendships. Plus, that ain't the goal.

The real work could help facilitate a widespread healing process unlike anything this country has ever seen. And thankfully, the real work can be initiated without the cooperation or participation of crack-ers who are not yet ready to be a part of the process.

The real work won't appeal to everyone. The real work takes courage and a strong willingness to buck conformity. The real work requires people able to see the big picture. The real work can change this country. If you've read this far, you are very likely ready to participate in the real work, Radical Forgiveness.

Before going deeper into Radical Forgiveness, please be mindful of my previous assertion that souls are complicit in higher-level healing opportunities. It might still sound crazy, I know. Who would volunteer to be beaten or shot in the name of healing America? No one consciously makes that decision; however, souls decide to do things for the collective good all the time and will continue to be a part of the process that facilitates Black people being safe in America.

Of course, no one in a human body can ever know for sure, but I strongly believe in the mission of souls and the existence of circumstances where they are brought together for sacred healing experiences that human eyes simply cannot fathom. Radical Forgiveness includes that premise.

So, what is Radical Forgiveness? Coined by the late Colin Tipping, it's a spiritual process that takes forgiveness to a whole new level. It rests on the foundation that we're spiritual beings having a human experience and that our souls are complicit in the healing we experience as humans.

Radical Forgiveness posits that there are no coincidences and that relationships present the ideal space for confronting the unhealed aspects of ourselves as they're reflected back to us by the people whose presence in our lives evoke the most visceral response. In intimate relationships, Radical Forgiveness helps people navigate seemingly insurmountable hurdles threatening marriages, parent/child connections, sibling stuff and more. The process involves shifting from victimhood to enlightenment and frees people to live happy, healthy and abundant lives.

From a collective perspective, the benefits are even more pronounced since the work being done by a group must also include each individual making a commitment to first embrace Radical Forgiveness on a personal level.

Since the personal embodiment of Radical Forgiveness informs its effectiveness at the collective level, it's essential that anyone willing to participate in the group process first apply the process personally.

A light, but effective approach examines the way crack'ers' antics infuriate us the same way we would examine why we have pet peeves. Pet peeves resonate so deeply because they remind us of something unresolved in our own lives. They remind us that some action others take gets us riled up because it triggers something we feel some kind of way about.

The solution isn't to avoid the pet peeves. The solution is to heal my response to the pet peeve so that it no longer resonates. For example, judgmental people used to irk the fuck out of me. When I realized how judgmental I was and did some work to release it, first of all, I encountered fewer judgmental people. But when I did come across someone judging others, it became far more fascinating than irritating.

So, as it relates to racial dynamics, does it piss you off when "Karens" call the police on an innocent Black person?

From a personal perspective, how are you policing yourself? How are you depriving yourself of rights to move freely in the world? (Whether you accept my theory or not, I encourage you to at least explore it and ask yourself the questions. You might be surprised at what you discover.)

Does it severely aggravate you when police officers racially profile Black people? Does it make your blood boil when they make assumptions about a person and put that person in a box based on their appearance?

From a personal perspective, how are you profiling yourself? How have you put yourself in a box as it relates to your ability to fully be yourself? As it relates to achieving your dreams and goals?

The way that crack-ers' treatment of others most infuriates you is the area you can gain the most benefit from personally. I already know what you're thinking – the experience that most infuriates you is when they kill Black people. Mine, too.

Stay with me here and consider how you've figuratively killed any aspect of your being. Have you given up on important dreams or goals? Are you playing small and going through the motions without really honoring who you are authentically? Are you alive but not really living?

When another crack-er shows their ass, process the experience. If it's tragic, grieve the loss of the Black person, pray for the family, get angry, feel what you need to feel, then do the work to identify how you've treated yourself in ways that possibly parallel what most angers you about the tragic incident.

To the extent that you've deprived yourself of opportunities to live freely as a citizen of the world, how much of it is due to your acceptance of crack-ers' beliefs about you? How much internalized oppression is guiding your perception of yourself and what you're capable of? How does internalized oppression guide the way you treat other Black people?

Systemic racism is real, but there are Black people who live freely, unrestrained by this country's efforts to limit their freedom. There are Black people whose consciousness isn't impacted by racism because they have consciously removed it from their radar.

In 1931, Abdullah was an Ethiopian rabbi who was also metaphysician Neville Goddard's mentor during a period in this country that Black people were brutally subjugated and controlled by threats or actual acts of violence. Yet, Abdullah moved through the world unharmed, totally aligned with his spiritual nature and oblivious to White people's fears and misperceptions about him. Brother man is said to have been an opera lover and would walk up in there, sit on one of the first few rows and enjoy the performance!

As it relates to radical forgiveness, all relationships, individually and collectively, present opportunities to heal, grow, evolve. But the work to heal, grow and evolve must be completed by the person desiring the healing, growth and evolving.

It always goes back to self, whether a one-on-one relationship or within the framework of a group. Identifying the emotions that arise within oneself when certain situations occur is an excellent guide to the work necessary for healing, growth and evolving.

As it relates to Black people navigating the healing process through the lens of racism, humongous power exists to radically shift consciousness and facilitate unimaginable levels of freedom.

Black people who subconsciously wait for crack-ers' behavior to change for them (Black people) to experience freedom and peace give up their power. Forcing crack-ers to change is futile. Expecting them to take the lead on fulfilling America's potential isn't what the playbook calls for. There's a role for them to play but taking the lead ain't it.

Besides, we've been dealing with this for centuries! While their behavior in some regards has changed, recent years indicate that the country takes big steps forward only to find itself hurtling backwards because the approaches employed are limited and include attacking the problem at the level of the problem.

Attempting to solve a problem at the level of the problem keeps the problem front and center. Any movement as it relates to the problem is around it, or beneath it, which could feel productive, but doesn't actually achieve lasting results.

Rising above the problem and using high level spiritual tools to dig deep and do the kind of sacred work true transformation requires is key. This is the kind of work that takes people out of their heads and into their hearts. It's the kind of work that requires taking a look at the big picture. It's the kind of work that needs renewed minds.

In a symbiotic manner, the freer Black people become of their own volition, the less sway crack'ers' have over their well-being. And the less sway crack-ers' have over Black people, the more likely crack-ers are to heal.

(To learn more and participate in the radical forgiveness process, go to www.understandingcrack-ers.com).

"I Wish I Knew How It Would Feel to Be Free"
Billy Taylor (performed by Nina Simone)

I wish I knew how
It would feel to be free
I wish I could break
All the chains holding me
I wish I could say
All the things that I should say
Say 'em loud say 'em clear
For the whole round world to hear

I wish I could share
All the love that's in my heart
Remove all the bars
That keep us apart
I wish you could know
What it means to be me
Then you'd see and agree
That every man should be free

I wish I could give
All I'm longin' to give
I wish I could live
Like I'm longin' to live
I wish I could do
All the things that I can do
Though I'm way overdue
I'd be starting anew.

Well I wish I could be like a bird in the sky
How sweet it would be
If I found I could fly
I'd soar to the sun
And look down at the sea
And I sing 'cause I know
How it feels to be free

Chapter 9

THE UNSTOPPABLE SOULS OF BLACK FOLKS

Crack-ers' relentless efforts to annihilate Black people have continued for centuries. Their psychotic, maniacal treatment of enslaved Africans, the ruthless, cold-blooded atrocities they inflicted upon freed Blacks seeking to create lives for themselves and their families, the unbridled jealousy and psychotic obsession to destroy Black Wall Street and other Black meccas are all behaviors stemming from people who have no idea who they really are. Crack-ers' seemingly insatiable desire to destroy Black people is not simply a historical reality, it's a contemporary blot stubbornly persisting in 2022.

African Americans have weathered an overwhelming onslaught of relentless thuggery thanks to our own country. We've endured ruthless violence, vast strategic messaging meant to undermine worthiness, the divesting of liberties readily shared with others, redlining, mass incarceration, voter suppression, encountering major disparities in virtually every U.S. system, yet Black folk have STILL managed to excel because Black folk cannot be stopped. The level of excellence this remarkable group of people has been able to manifest, despite crack-ers' obstinate attempts to deny them life itself is utterly astonishing.

Sure, there are segments of the country where internalized oppression has profoundly stunted our brothers' and sisters' potential, but overall, that Black people have gotten as far as we have is a testament to a people committed to reaching our God-given potential. But despite how magnificent our progression, we have really only scratched the surface of our greatness.

How do we get beyond the surface? How do we move past external obstacles designed to limit our greatness? How do we encourage each other to step outside of comfort zones we've been convinced we belong in? How do we change the narrative that defines how far we go collectively?

We begin by acknowledging that there is nothing inherently wrong with us. And then we recognize that as the primary focus of America's hatred and violence, and the group least likely to receive its compassion, it stands to reason that we have been adversely impacted emotionally, physically, mentally, financially and psychologically.

It's no surprise that our people have the highest blood pressure, suffer the most heart attacks, are infected with HIV at higher rates, are paid less money, pay more for mortgages when they are approved and pull up last in a host of other socioeconomic and health categories. The mind-body connection is real and stress places a tremendous burden on the body as well as the mind's ability to function at peak performance.

Centuries of relentless racism exact a burdensome toll on the collective well-being of the people being targeted. James Baldwin said, "To be a Negro in this country and to be relatively conscious is to be in a rage almost all the time." And it's true. But we cannot afford to be in a rage all the time because of its impact on us, its impact on our mental health, our physical health, our ability to experience joy and our capacity to prosper.

People undoubtedly rise above it, but unlike other groups that can put all their focus on thriving, Black people's energy has typically been diverted to surviving racial bullshit.

Consider that in the 1960s, White people held seven times more wealth than Black people. Time is marching on, and some Blacks have prospered in unimaginable ways, but widespread Black prosperity is stagnant because decades later, that figure is virtually the same with White people having 6.9 times more wealth.

We did not just wake up lagging behind because we're not capable of keeping up. Post traumatic slavery syndrome is real and is a predominant underlying factor in virtually every aspect of our lives. In addition to navigating life's normal ups and downs, as African Americans, we have residual baggage, some of which we're completely unaware of, influencing our health, relationships, finances and success. It's also shaping the way we think, the way we act and the way we treat ourselves and each other.

Consider the personal idiosyncrasies most everyone has to navigate with parents, grandparents and other family members. Some grew up with an alcoholic father or a people-pleasing mother. Maybe poverty was a constant factor or control issues were prevalent.

Now compound those realities with racial dynamics our elder family members likely navigated at the time, circumstances that kept them boxed in, unable to pursue what they needed to heal, to grow, to prosper. Think about the limiting beliefs some accepted regarding who they could be and what they could do as African Americans and how those limiting beliefs unwittingly seeped into how they raised their children.

As a matter of survival, our ancestors adapted their behavior, some of which has been passed on through generational patterns, as well as through DNA. The restrictive practices and laws the nation enacted to deprive Black people, keep them struggling and without the provisions everyone else was afforded impacted families then, and the long-term ramifications of those injustices are still felt now. Black people have struggled to survive in this country.

But we're not meant to struggle indefinitely.

Author Gay Hendricks says, "Our species in general had grown accustomed to pain and adversity through millennia of struggle. We knew how to feel bad. We had millions of nerve connections devoted to registering pain, and we had a huge expanse of territory in the center of our bodies dedicated to feeling fear."

He's referring to humanity as a whole, but I think his statement is most relevant to African Americans. We're so accustomed to being discriminated against, so used to seeing Black bodies destroyed, so weary about protecting our individual and collective safety and well-being in virtually every mainstream public space that the idea of ALL of us living freely, securely, manifesting joyful, abundant experiences, frolicking, and thriving CONSISTENTLY can feel unrealistic and unattainable.

Struggling has been such an integral part of our reality that we *expect* to struggle – even if there is an easier path to freedom. In his masterpiece of a book, *The Big Leap*, Hendricks explains that all people have what he coined, an "upper limit problem." When we are pursuing better in any aspect of our lives, if we have not dealt with our upper limit problem, we will somehow sabotage our efforts so that we do not manifest too much success, or too much happiness, or too much goodness.

We hit a ceiling and default back to what's familiar, a space in our lives that's easier to manage than this new territory where success, or a better relationship, or happiness or improved health, more money, etc. exist. We've trained ourselves so effectively that sliding back into familiar, albeit mediocre, territory feels justified.

Each of us has an individual upper limit problem based on the life journey we've traveled with our families and childhood experiences. Personal upper limit problems could take the form of shrinking to appease a relative who might be uncomfortable with you succeeding, or some limiting narrative you received in childhood that continues to play on repeat in your mind when you're pursuing important goals. Upper limit problems can run the gamut, but what they have in common is the power to stop you from excelling beyond a certain level. It's like having your own personal glass ceiling.

Well, on a collective level, Black people have an upper limit problem orchestrated by America's cracked consciousness manifesting as systemic racism, brutality, blatant and subtle discrimination perpetuated for centuries. It's a generalized premise that does not limit everyone, however, as a whole, African Americans have unwittingly internalized limiting beliefs about who we are and what we're capable of. We've grown so accustomed to life in America being a struggle that we've established self-imposed limitations that kick in even if the exterior barriers we anticipate are not present.

The human dynamic that African Americans traverse makes it imperative to plug into the aspect of our existence that cannot be controlled by humans. Relinquishing the belief that America defines who you are and what you can or cannot accomplish is essential to thriving. Realizing that you are individualized expressions of Infinite Intelligence and are therefore unlimited is absolutely critical to releasing your subconscious allegiance to struggling.

I'm repeating this because we need to internalize this truth.

We are not meant to struggle indefinitely.

We are not meant to lag behind all other groups in every damn category of life. We are not meant to constantly be on guard, searching for and expecting racism to rear its head when we're pursuing any endeavor or simply living. We are not meant to play small or settle, convinced that a bigger, better life is beyond our reach. We're not meant to, but as long as we are primarily governed by the *human* dynamic of our existence, we will remain limited by its constraints.

This is delicate territory that could sound incredibly unrealistic. How do we behave as though racism isn't real? How do we circumvent the systemic obstacles created to trip us up?

By intentionally giving those aspects of America far less of your energy. If you're drawn to racist news stories or social media posts, shift your focus to uplifting content about Black people inventing fascinating shit or Black babies dancing or Black men surfing or Black families farming. Anything with Black people thriving.

This isn't burying your head in the sand. If there's news you need to know about, trust me you'll hear it. The main point is we don't have to monitor America's racism, brutality and unfairness, especially knowing our subconscious takes what we give it literally and does its job to manifest more of it. A much better use of our energy is stepping out of our comfort zones and living our best lives.

While we definitely play a role in facilitating the healing of cracked consciousness by sending crack-ers positive energy, holding our breath until they change is not a part of the equation.

Also, it might be the hardest work we've ever done, but we must overhaul our expectations, because ultimately, what we expect, we experience. We've got to commit to completing internal work on a large scale, doing it FUBU style and celebrating each other for going within. With enough of us doing the work individually, upleveling how we manifest collectively is a given.

By embarking on a widespread SPIRITUAL RENAISSANCE, we can make manifesting our best the rule and not the exception. We can claim our true place, not only in the U.S., but in the world by embracing that our souls are limitless as individualized expressions of the UNIVERSE.

Another facet of our existence that needs our loving attention is managing what lands in our mental storehouse. Subconsciously, Black people have an overwhelming storehouse of historical and contemporary memories, lived and observed, informing perception of self, each other and life in these United States.

Enslaved ancestors' lacerated backs, Mike Brown lying lifeless in the street. Black bodies hanging. Little children ripped from mothers' exhausted arms, Sandy Bland disrespected and humiliated. High powered water, hosed onto dignified, freedom-seeking bodies. Police officers' timeless, frenzied, state sanctioned night sticks cracking Black skulls, "patriotic" bullets tearing into innocent Black skin. Philando Castile perishing before his family's eyes. Eric Garner's breathless pleading. Tamir Rice's brief childhood. Breonna Taylor executed.

Each of the incidents likely brought to mind an image stored in your subconscious. Lasting weighty impressions leaving less space for lighter memories, for dreaming big dreams, or downloading celestial messaging beckoning us higher. But we must. We must dream big dreams and download the messages because we're the ones to manifest them. We truly are our ancestors' hopes and dreams.

To facilitate the collective healing we need and deserve, we must limit what gets added to those images. Trust me, I understand what you might be feeling about this. I've felt it, too.

We feel obligated to view every documented atrocity and could feel guilty if we don't. We feel that bearing witness somehow validates our allegiance to the victims. It doesn't. Our love for Black lives isn't lessened by choosing not to observe their traumatic demise.

Documenting the atrocities has been a necessary part of the evolutionary energy to eliminate the behavior, but we're the only people compelled to view video after video of their people being slaughtered. We cannot afford to continue. For the sake of our mental and emotional health, we cannot afford to continue. We've already seen enough to last several lifetimes. And it's time to take a more intentional approach to minimizing the harm inflicted upon our psyche.

We can hold our beloveds in our hearts and add our energy, resources and actions to the calls for justice, but self-care for Black people must include standing guard at the gateway of our subconscious minds. To protect our mental health, we must increasingly turn off the TV and shut down social media when images of yet another Black body killed without reason takes the viral journey.

More than anyone else, Black people must embrace their spiritual nature. Must own that they're spiritual beings having this human experience to repel the relentless racial mayhem. Must plug into Infinite Intelligence, be fueled by its vast, unlimited power, welcome its infiltration into the subconscious, and very deliberately replace trauma with triumph. Be in this world, not of it. Present but untouchable, moving through the human experience as pure unfiltered light.

And we must also give up the fight without giving up our expectations for change. The primary strategy to combat racism has been fighting against it. We've been doing that for how long now?

That approach yields marginal progress at best and cannot facilitate the type of transformation Black people need to thrive. The approach that *could* lead to the type of transformation needed to elevate Black people in every aspect of life does not include fighting against racism or trying to compel White people to behave a certain way.

Spiritual law is spiritual law, and it cares not for back stories. It doesn't care how justified anger feels. It does not analyze why we think what we think, it simply responds to it.

Thoughts are things. They're powerful and they manifest into reality. The things we focus on most, the subject matter most prevalent among the average of 60,000 thoughts we think daily is what shows up as our lives. So even though it might feel productive to fight racism, as long as we're thinking about how to fight racism, we will continue to manifest experiences that need us to fight racism. The way our subconscious minds take our thoughts literally guarantees that thinking about fighting racism keeps us fighting racism.

We don't create peace by thinking about war. We don't spread love by focusing on hate. To achieve goals, one of the most effective success principles we can adopt is focusing on what we want, not what we don't want. Visualization works. If we can't see it in our minds, we cannot manifest it. As it relates to racism, the way to dismantle it is not by thinking about ways to eliminate it, but by visualizing life without it.

Imagining racially tinged experiences without the racially tinged components. Imagine police officers serving and protecting. Imagine walking into stores shopping freely. Imagine applying for loans and receiving them with favorable rates. Imagine being hired at your dream job. Imagine voting easily at your precinct or conveniently online from the comfort of your home. Imagine living your best life in every conceivable way.

The foundational shift necessary for visualizing a racist-free America requires that Black people make embracing themselves as spiritual beings an urgent priority. It requires unplugging from the unlevel playing field with its constantly changing rules and plugging into the field of Infinite Intelligence with its unlimited Divine energy and using it to manifest better health, increased wealth, successful businesses, and the lives they're meant to live.

We can actually think our way into increased power, better health, more peace, expanded joy.

Chapter 10

THIS LAND IS YOUR LAND, THIS LAND IS MY LAND

Blacks must take full ownership of America as their country. Not to take it away from anyone, but to fully embody it as THEIR country. Our ancestors built it, we are full legal citizens and we have as much right to claim it as anyone else. And our right to claim ownership is not contingent upon anyone else's approval or permission.

Many Black people feel subtly disenfranchised and an unspoken doubt that the country is really theirs. With the revolting ongoing abuse, deprivation of basic rights, attempts to suppress their full participation in the democratic process, constant efforts to them deny access to the "American Dream," and more, why should they claim a country that clearly doesn't want them?

It's time for a major shift in perspective. From feeling like foreigners in our own land, feeling displaced because of our origin story and reluctant to stake our claim, to embracing that regardless of how it started, we have more than earned the right to all benefits of our citizenry in the United States of America. This is as much our country as it is anyone else's.

The full embodiment of that truth can produce a monumental shift in consciousness, a shift that's necessary for our freedom. So much of what blocks us from excelling is rooted in the limitations imposed by racism. The floundering feeling resulting from not feeling like "true" Americans coupled with not knowing the exact origin of our ancestors produces a scattered energy that greatly impacts our ability to excel and manifest fully. The Universe trusts that what we give most of our attention is what we want to experience, so when we ask, it delivers. Scattered energy produces scattered results.

Ultimately, fully accepting that we're spiritual beings having a human experience is vital, however, acknowledging that WHERE we're having this human experience is by Divine Design is a critical component and a key to our liberation. The souls of Black folk in America are instrumental to the elevation of this country. The elevation, however, must first occur *within* Black folk independent of participation with or from White people.

The unspoken, unwritten dichotomy Black people face includes an invisible asterisk next to their status as citizens. The intellectual awareness of citizenry as evidenced by birth certificates lacks the soulful embrace of citizenry other nationalities fully enjoy by virtue of mutual love between them and their country.

Referring to ourselves as **AFRICAN** Americans is an attempt to fill a void attached to the questionable status as citizens in a land hell bent on rejecting us. Adding "African" to "American" provides a sense of belonging even if we've never visited Africa. For those who have, the connection takes on a different meaning.

Black people's lifeline to Africa is sacred and should be revered. It's a lifeline that must be cultivated and appreciated. A lifeline that should include vibrant, intentional celebrations, complete with visits that commemorate the sacred connection to ancestral energy.

In this country, there's a part of our consciousness with invisible brakes on its ability to fully expand as long as our primary focus is on the human experience. For us, the human experience in America is fraught with struggle, multifaceted assaults, being on the defensive as a matter of survival and the cultural belief in working twice as hard as others whose success comes easier.

But there's a powerful spiritual reckoning poised to unfold in and through Black people that solves stubborn issues long blocking our progress while also unleashing pent up energy celebrating our status as American citizens.

From a spiritual perspective, Black people are expressions of the Universe, and our place in this country is Divinely ordered. We are chosen to lead the United States to its destiny – because our presence here is intrinsically tied to the country's inability to align with its inherent greatness. We are a mirror to the country, reflecting what it needs to heal.

Souls do not die. Their journey is endless. Their energy continues and informs other incarnated souls to whom they're inherently connected. From their vantage point, they know things we don't know. They realize the easiest paths to our freedom even when we keep tripping over self-imposed obstacles.

Souls whisper timeless wisdom to many souls, but they respect free will. As much as our ancestors want us to listen up and take heed, they will not force anything on us. They keep whispering because they know some of us are listening.

For earthly souls to hear their messages requires an intention to welcome sacred truth. It needs people committing to a daily spiritual practice where sacred silence and going within via meditation are foundational.

As it relates to the souls that were kidnapped and brought across the Middle Passage, those that made it to America and those whose journey ended at sea, we are the souls to whom they're connected, and they want to see us ascend the limited circumstances that could continue for generations if we keep on doing the same things, expecting different results. They want us to love on each other like our lives depend on it. They want us to practice compassion, exercise patience and see the best in every Black person we encounter.

The souls of our ancestors want us to guarantee that their horrendous experience was not in vain. They're watching us, wanting us to free ourselves from the mental shackles. They're saying, "we didn't choose to be there, but now that you are, please live as fully and freely as you can!"

Our ability to be *in* America, but not *of* America as it relates to its systemic efforts to oppress is critical. To fully embody our Truth as spiritual beings divinely assigned to this country for a reason – namely its healing. America cannot heal without us. But while it's healing, we must live and live fully.

The soul work America must complete includes reconciling the crack between its Truth and how it has behaved for centuries, but here's the rub. That soul work must be completed independent of any obligation to treat Black people better. Focusing on how it treats us could provide a gateway to profound healing but treating Black people better should not be the goal of America's healing. That would be an externally focused agenda that doesn't allow for the substantive healing the country desperately needs.

America must become healthy for the sake of being healthy. It must learn how to do the right thing even if no one is watching. When the nation is functioning from its collective truth, from its true greatness, all its inhabitants, citizens, immigrants, visitors, anyone stepping foot on American soil would be treated with dignity and respect. Treating Black people better will be a natural result and can serve as the litmus test for gauging America's progress.

It's time. Black people feel an insatiable longing to belong to a place where unconditional acceptance, and their fellow Americans' genuine desire to see them thrive comes naturally. Black people deserve to have that experience.

HBCUs (Historically Black Colleges and Universities) provide that feeling. They offer safe spaces for Black folk to be themselves in atmospheres of unconditional acceptance with a natural expectation for Black people to excel. The fervent fights for HBCUs' survival are to retain this utopic experience in a country where being an American citizen can feel loaded with conflicting loyalties.

No such conflict exists at HBCUs. The vibrant, liberating, full on joy reverberating at an HBCU and all of its functions, especially football games, is unlike ANY collective public experience Black people have in any other aspect of life as an American citizen.

We are meant to experience that HBCU type of vibrancy as American citizens but it's an experience that must be cultivated from the inside-out, independent of involvement or permission from White people. Regardless of the state of America, Black people must decide to live fully.

Online trends like #blackmenfrolicking, #blackboyjoy, #blackgirlmagic, #blackgirlsrock and #blackmensmiling are Black people reminding each other of their right to frolic, experience joy and magic and smiling because this country has done such an effective job of making Black people feel undeserving of liberties White people feel free to engage in all the fucking time. What's vitally important for Black people to understand is how absolutely imperative it is to give *themselves* permission to frolic, experience joy, smile, prosper, thrive, make mistakes, be goofy, fail, succeed and LIVE full out without anyone's approval.

It is no exaggeration that most Black people think about or in some way encounter racial dynamics involving White people every day. Whether directly or indirectly, it's a natural part of being Black in America. And because it's such a part of our consciousness, collectively, Black people's consciousness plays a significant role in the country's racial dynamics.

Black people are not powerless. Far from it, however the type of power most instrumental in manifesting the transformation America is due comes not from marching, protesting or even voting. All are significant and play a role, however, the power that will result in the transformation of the United States of America is Divine power expressed through Black people.

It's the power flowing from Black people's awareness that they're spiritual beings having a human experience, but also that White people with a crack in their consciousness are also spiritual beings having a human experience.

It's the power that Martin Luther King advocated because it flows from unconditional love.

PRAYER FOR AMERICA'S GREATNESS

Infinite Intelligence is unlimited. It is love in its purest form. Infinite Intelligence pours forth in, through and as every aspect of life. It is Life itself. It is the only power and wisdom shaping America into its highest and best form. It is the foundation of America's greatness.

We are individualized expressions of this sacred Life. We, Black people, We, White people, We, all people, are unique pinpoints through which the Universe expresses Itself. We now open ourselves fully to its goodness and to its love.

This Divine Presence now activates in the hearts and minds of Americans. It now heals cracked consciousness, invigorates, renews and blesses all. It manifests now as peace, as joy, as love and abundance.

With tremendous gratitude, we give thanks for a new America. With profound thankfulness, we envision a beautiful nation amidst a world that works for all.
With immense appreciation for our ancestors and loving anticipation for our descendants, we embrace this now moment of expansive power.

We now release this mighty prayer back to Infinite Intelligence, knowing that it has the power to create anything we imagine and more. We release this prayer and stand in the truth of this awareness that we are One.
We release this prayer, trusting that all is well as America's greatness unfolds into full manifestation.

Amen. Ashe. And so it is.

IMAGINE
John Lennon

Imagine there's no heaven
It's easy if you try
No hell below us
Above us only sky
Imagine all the people
Living for today... Aha-ah...

Imagine there's no countries
It isn't hard to do
Nothing to kill or die for
And no religion, too
Imagine all the people
Living life in peace... You...

You may say I'm a dreamer
But I'm not the only one
I hope someday you'll join us
And the world will be as one

Imagine no possessions
I wonder if you can
No need for greed or hunger
A brotherhood of man
Imagine all the people
Sharing all the world... You...

You may say I'm a dreamer
But I'm not the only one
I hope someday you'll join us
And the world will live as one

ABOUT
THE AUTHOR

Michelle is a New Thought spiritual practitioner. She served as a prayer chaplain at two of Miami's most powerful New Thought spiritual centers, Unity on the Bay and the Universal Truth Center. She is currently a member of Celebration Spiritual Center, located in Brooklyn.

A graduate of Florida State University with a degree in sociology, Michelle has written two books for the child welfare system, *The ABCs of Authentic Work with Families* and *Seven Steps to Strengthen Your Family*.

She is also the author of *The Sisterhood Exchange*, and several books on the topic of worthiness, *Worthy, Are You Worthy?*, and *Sis, You're Worth It: Seven Ideas for Manifesting Your Best Life*.

The mother of three and grandmother of two loves dancing, live music, reading, great movies and relaxing on the beach with delicious wine and a page-turner.

An inspirational speaker, Michelle connects with her listeners' souls and helps them expand their views easily, with grace and spiritual dignity. She truly believes with her heart and soul, that the United States can be great.

Learn more at www.understandingcrack-ers.com.

RECOMMENDED RESOURCES

BOOKS

The New Jim Crow
Michelle Alexander

The Power of Decision
Raymond Charles Barker

Post Traumatic Slave Syndrome
Dr. Joy DeGruy

You Can Heal Your Life
Louise Hay

Sis, You're Worth It
Michelle Hollinger

30 Day Mental Diet
Willis Kinnear

My Life After Hate
Arno Michaelis

Seat of the Soul
Gary Zukav

NEW THOUGHT SPIRITUAL CENTERS

Agape International Spiritual Center
www.agapelive.com

Celebration Spiritual Center
www.celebrationsc.org

Unity on the Bay
www.unityonthebay.org.

Universal Truth Center
www.utruthcenter.org

Christ Universal Temple
www.cutemple.org

Understanding Principles for Better Living
www.upchurch.org

Unity of Sacramento
www.unityofsacramento.org

Spiritual Life Center
www.slcworld.org